Paper Stars

Kristine Ciraulo

Copyright © 2022 by Kristine Ciraulo
All rights reserved.

part one

Once upon a time,
there was a sad and twisted fairy tale.

It was ours.

And it was far too broken to be beautiful.

Me:
A small-town girl,
searching for a way out
and dreaming of castles in the clouds.

You:
A false prince,
with a black heart
and a hole in your soul.

Poison kisses.
Empty wishes.

Midnight brought only darkness.

My kingdom,
disenchanted.

Make-believe love
in a world of lies.

I was lost in a place
that never was.

In the end?
It ended.

Like all true endings do.

No more chances for second chances.
No more trying just one more time.

Giving up.
Because there was nothing left to give.

And it hurt.
The way all broken things do.

Whether it's a promise
or a heart
or a life.

When they break,
it hurts.

And it's dark and cold and empty.
Nothing left but shadows.

And the end. . .
it ended.

And I walk with ghosts.

Dreams are just lies
the night tells.

So when I wake up in the dark
crying from some leftover dream about you,
I hold tightly to my tears
and try to slip back into sleep.

Because the only place I can find you now
is in the shadows of my dreams.

Only the mornings are honest,
when I wake up
and remember that you're gone.

There's a hole in the world
where you used to be.

And I can't breathe
where there is nothing.

I am haunted by the truth
and taunted by the empty spaces
in the places where my heart used to be.

I have an invisible life
that only I can see

Because that life?
It never really happened.

It just sits quietly
beside the one that actually did.

My invisible life.

The one where you stayed.

The one where you loved me
like I loved you.

I blame the night when I can't sleep.
I blame the dark when I can't see.
I blame the air when I can't breathe.

I curse a god I don't believe in
when I can't quiet the screams in my head.

But I cherish all my scars.
The ones you left behind.

My only reminder
of how it felt to be alive.

I am haunted by the echoes
of your pleas for absolution.

The landscape of my life,
once lush and thriving,
is a blackened ruin.

The wind that once carried
our beautiful music
now only sings of deception.

The stars grieve,
dim and heavy
with hushed tales of betrayal.

And the moon weeps softly.

I long for stillness
in this choking chaos.

But I swallow my screams.
Some stories are best left untold.

Stone hearts show no mercy
and it is here
I find my silence.

Boo.
Guess who?

Can you see my reflection
crying silently behind you?

I tiptoe through the swirling gray fog
and in the dim spaces
between your thoughts.

I am the ghost
of lifetimes past.

These empty rooms
are silent tombs.

Life has gone on without us.

It is here that I will whisper my truths
and you can scream your lies.

Then we will see
on which side the echo lands.

I died the day you left.

It's true,
I'm still breathing.

But as everyone knows. . .

there
are
a
thousand
ways
to
die.

Cheers to the unbroken,
who live in a world
where hope blooms wild,
like roses.

The ones who think
that happiness will be found
just around the next corner.

Who can still close the gaps
in a world ripped wide open.

Eyes that see the flowers
instead of graveyards.

Hearts that don't seek out
the shadowed places.

The ones who still believe
that love doesn't always have to hurt.

I raise my glass and wish them well.

But I laugh too.

Because I am nothing like them.

I crave the dark.

And I have earned each and every one
of my drunken scars.

Now that I'm gone,
do you even remember
that I was ever here at all?

Do thoughts of us linger
in the quiet places of your mind?

Do memories of what we had,
and what we were,
whisper to you
from the dark corners
of an empty house?

Or were they erased
by time and ambivalence?

I vanished like smoke.

We are in that place.

That dangerous place.

Where hope and fear and love and hate
get tangled up together.

The place where I learned
that a scream is still a scream,
even when it's disguised as a whisper.

Night was the only place you
knew how to love me.

And it was there we came alive.

Dancing under the stars,
young and free and wild.

Believing in the magic of midnight.

But morning always came too soon,
and with the light
would come the truth.

And you would disappear,
running off to chase the sun.

While I was left
chasing you.

I wait.

I wait for the time
when the wind screams,
and the night sky holds no stars.

I wait for the time
when the golden light of summer
shatters like glass,
and the air turns gray and mean.

I wait for winter.

Icy and bleak,
when you're cold and tired
and scared of being alone.

I wait.

Because that is when
I know you'll come back to me.

It's hard,
loving a ghost.

You grew up so fast,
you never found anything
to believe in.

I wish you would have believed in me.

I wish you could have believed in us.

You stole everything from me that day.

That long ago day,
when you went away.

Everything I had.
Everything I was.

I would have gladly given it all to you.

My heart.
My life.
My world.

You left nothing behind
but bones and ashes.

We have come this way before.

All hail the King of Thieves.

Every once in a while,
we find a fragile harmony,
in the middle of all this madness.

But then you call forth
your armies of demons
and they drive it back.

Back behind the chaos,
where we can't hear the music anymore.

Beautiful songs,
drowned out by the beating black wings
of a legion of a thousand monsters.

I try to stand strong and push them away,
but I grow weary of the fight.

I'll take them on some other day.

Our story
may have been written in the stars.

But it's told only by the scars
you left behind.

You were just so damn beautiful.

Bright and sharp,
like the icy cold steel
of a razor's edge.

And I learned the hard way
that you were just as deadly.

It's true, you were dangerous,
but my wounds have always been
self-inflicted

We got so good at pretending,
that we actually believed we could be
what we thought we were.

Living in a bright, make-believe world
where the lies always tasted sweeter than the truth.

But when the light faded,
I was left all alone,
screaming in the darkness.

And in the end
I prayed to a god
who didn't even know my name.

And I got only silence in return.

I thought that I had finally protected myself.

From you.

But here I am again,
bruised and bleeding.

My walls, so carefully constructed,
proved to be no match
for the arsenal of weapons
you brought to our war.

And I'm lying on the ground,
crushed and broken in the rubble.

Out of options.
Out of time.
I surrender.

I am all sharp edges
and broken glass.

My heart, a map of scars,
left over from a time
when your words cut deeper
than my razor ever did.

We could have been so much more
than what we were.

But we didn't ever see it.

Because we were always too busy
waging war on one another.

And when it was finally over,
it was too late.

We had become casualties
of ourselves.

Duty bound,
by a history I didn't write.

I tried to say
what I needed to say.

But I never could find the words
that would have saved us.

All that time together,
we never fell apart.

Until we did.

But even now,
I keep coming back
to this broken place.

Prepared to fight a war
I am never meant to win.

Our story lingers in the air.

Heavy.
But vague like smoke.

We wrote our history
from the outside, in.

It began with the tomorrows.
It ended with the yesterdays.

All that's left here
is the end of us

No wonder we couldn't make it work,
when everything about our story
was so mixed up.

I wish we could have started
what we finished.

All that time
I spent watching you.

Drowning,
at the bottom of a bottle.

Trying to heal
your broken soul.

If only you could have just let go,
and looked up at the stars.

If only you would have just reached out,
and taken my hand.

I wanted forever.
You gave me for now.

Because you were never able
to give me anything else.

And I accepted it.
Each and every time.

Because it was something.
And something was always better than nothing.

And it was OK.

Until some pretty new plaything
would come along
and catch your eye
and your heart.

And I would take my place
at the back of the line,
hope always hiding the truth.

Time was my only luxury.

I would wait.

Wait until you came back to me,
after one of your shiny golden butterflies
had flown away and left you all alone.

Then you would look for me
and reach for my hand,
which was already reaching for yours.

Because I was always so good
at catching you when you fell.

It was hard.
Loving you.

Hard to look at you
and see you staring off in the other direction.

Hard to keep up
when you were always two steps ahead of me.

And when I saw how your smile
never reached your eyes.

Hard when your heart
didn't echo your words.

And when I realized
that I was a just a summer souvenir.

Hard when I finally understood
that something inside of you was broken,
and that nothing I could ever do
would fix it.

Loving you.
It made me small.

And I loved you more than you ever knew.

And I learned that love
would never be enough.

Yes.
Loving you was hard.

All those wasted years.

Pouring whiskey
over our sad hearts.

Speaking the language
of the young and broken.

Only the wind heard us crying.

We are living
a spectacular and beautiful lie.

We get so distracted by carnival games
and shiny trinkets,
that we forget about the damage
caused by the past we share.

We hide our broken hearts
behind silver-framed smiles on the mantle.

We keep our secrets
locked away in glass boxes with no keys.

The truth will probably catch up to us one day.

But for now,
let's just keep pretending.

It's all there.
In your eyes.

The truth.
The lies.
And everything in between.

The words we whisper.
And those we scream.

Some stories
will remain forever unfinished.

And some have endings
that were written
long before the beginnings.

And sometimes lives and loves
will break apart
no matter how beautiful they might have been.

Because no matter how hard we try
or how much we hope,
we can never rewrite
what has already been written.

You asked me to. . .

So I took your hand
and followed you into the dark place
beyond your heart.

It was there I heard
what I couldn't see.

And your truths became my lies,
tears in my tired eyes.

And when all was said and done,
I realized
that the only easy parts
were the good-byes.

We are slowly unraveling.

The rope connecting us
is growing thin and frayed.

There is nothing left to grab onto,
and I don't think it will hold us much longer.

One of us will need to let go,
in order to save the other.

Ready.
Your words are bullets,
raining down on me
faster than the speed of silence.

Aim.
I pray your hands are steady.
Shoot true and find my heart.

Fire.
I will be a willing victim
of you.

I lived my own life
and I made my own choices.

Throwing fistfuls of broken glass
from my stone house,
while trying to stay out of my own way.

I received a false pardon,
but I still couldn't save myself
from breaking into a million pieces.

I know that you loved me.
But only a little bit at a time.

A gift,
that came with a heavy price.

I kept it all with me.

The jagged parts,
The sharp pieces.

The things that hurt the most
were proof that it was real.

The secrets we carry
are heavier
than the truths that I bury.

Though I can hardly breathe
from the burden of either.

It seems that lies
are all that I can bear the weight of anymore.

I am the girl who was invisible.

I am all that ever was.
But I was never here.

I am infinite.
And I am nothing,

It's all there,
in your eyes.

Our truth.
My lies.
Your black heart.

And everything in between.

What was said.
And what wasn't.

The lure of a sharp knife beckons.

The winner will be
whose blade can cut the deepest.

We both know how this will end.

I am steel.
And I am made of glass.

I have stood and faced the fiercest storms,
with fire in my heart
and lightning in my hands.

Yet the look in your eyes
the day you left
shattered me into a million pieces.

Sing me a song
filled with empty words.

Tell me a story
made up of beautiful lies.

Give me nothing but make-believe
and happy endings.

For the truth grows old too quickly
and I'm exhausted by the silence.

Cracked glass,
and hands that don't seem to know
which direction to go anymore.

Midnight always strikes twice.

Broken clocks don't run backwards.
They just quit running altogether.

Here I am.
Killing time.

Tick Tock
It all stops.

You came from a place
of broken things.

No wings.

I'm so sorry
that I was never able
to teach you how to fly.

Crash and burn,
then burn some more.

It's all we've ever known.

We chose this life in the flames,
so what we live
is who we are.

If only we could stop
throwing gasoline on the fire,
and let a little rain come in through the window.

Sometimes I feel
like a ballerina in a music box
who has forgotten how to dance.

Faded red velvet walls,
and a tin can piano.

Day after day.
Spinning in endless circles.

Can't someone please just stop the music?

I gave you the fragile parts of me.
The ones that I knew could be broken.

Being with you leaves me bleeding.
And loving you is killing me.

But honestly,
it's the only thing
that has ever made me feel alive.

So go ahead and tear me apart,
and don't be gentle with my heart.

Because being numb inside
is far worse than dying
from you.

This can only end badly.

Make it my fault if you must.

I'm bruised and broken,
but only on the inside,
where no one else can see.

I leave it there.

Because pain is the only thing that's real.

And it's the only thing
I have left to feel.

Love was never meant for the weak.

Ours was such a mixed-up story.

Always on divergent paths.
Coming together just for a moment,
before spinning off in opposite directions.

I often wondered
if you were my journey
or my destination.

Maybe you were both.
Maybe you were neither

All I know
is that the wind turned me around
and I found myself lost
on a road to nowhere.

I knew my compass was broken
when I couldn't seem to find us anymore.

And nothing I ever did
could get me back
to where I was supposed to be going.

And in the end
we were free falling.

Because we never learned
how to fly.

I never once told you
how much I loved you.

The words would have been
an unfair burden for you to carry.

A responsibility too great
for me to ask you to bear.

So you went away,
never knowing.

And I set your heart free
while breaking my own.

You left me with a life of scars
that no one else can see.

Except for me.

Maps of a dangerous road
I must never travel on again.

Unless of course...

I look up one day
and see you standing there
with your crooked "come here" smile.

Then I might find myself
On that old familiar path again.

Just one last time...

I was the reason
you wouldn't go.

You were the reason
I couldn't stay.

We've gotten lost so many times
I don't know
if we can ever find our way back
to each other again.

You're in my blind spot,
and these strange roads
only lead me back to myself.

Some truths
are harder to accept than lies.

I learned this
on the day you left.

When you never looked back.
Not even once.

When I realized that everything
had meant nothing.

Going through the motions of living
while I'm dying inside.

I just want to sink
underwater,
and let the sea swallow my tears.

Or get lost
deep in the forest,
where the silence will drown out my screams.

Or run so hard that I can't breathe.
Just so I won't feel this crushing sadness
in my chest anymore.

Or maybe I'll just jump.

Jump out into the black empty sky
and fly.

So I won't have to feel anything,
ever again.

Don't worry.
((They say))

There's someone else out there.

You'll find someone new.
Just give it time.

But how can that be?

When time began with you
and ended with you.

How can that be?

When it was always you.
When it will only ever be you.

How can that be?

When I will spend the rest of my life
trying to find you again.

Holding hands,
as we walk along the beach.

We have created the illusion
of a life together.

But when we get too close to the water
our footprints are washed away
by the rising tides.

The path that led us here vanishes,
but we pretend not to notice.

We pretend we aren't living
a sad and beautiful lie.

We pretend that this is more
than smoke and mirrors.

We pretend.

Words leave echoes behind.

And we couldn't ever change that
no matter how hard we tried.

Things we wished we hadn't said
but could never take back.

And the silence that remained
was far more deafening
than any scream ever was.

I'm tangled up in memories.

Wrapped up so tightly
I can barely breathe.

They drag me down,
and won't let me go.

I'm drowning.

Lost so deep
in this maze of yesterdays
that I can't find my way out
into tomorrow.

It got so heavy.
The US part of us.

Being together.
And how everything got so mixed up.

A familiar dance between strangers.

It got so heavy
that nothing would ever be the same again.

But then again,
nothing was ever the same to begin with.

A storm is raging.

Lightning cracks
and tears the sky apart.

The wind is wild,
ripping my hair
and drowning out my screams.

I can't feel my breath
in the air anymore.

Time on fire.

Memories lost
in this beautiful mess we made.

Was there ever really any quiet?

Or was I only dreaming
about a dream
about a dream?

Peace is a mirage.

Endless searching
for that elusive state of grace.

I wonder sometimes. . .

Would you still have slipped away
if I hadn't held on so tightly?

Or maybe I didn't hold on tight enough?

Maybe the call of darkness
was just too strong.

Did it scream out your name?
Or did it whisper?

Either way,
I couldn't keep you with me.

Hope was always just out of reach.

Despair stayed by your side,
no matter how fast you ran.

But you never stopped running.

And you were lost to me.

We were like stars
that had been shaken from the sky.

Everything strange
and unfamiliar.

Trapped in a glass prison.

Floating in the strong currents,
we were swept out to sea and lost.

Life in a bottle.

You were always everything
that I ever wanted.

But you were never anything
that I ever needed.

I thought that I could love you enough
for the both of us.

I'm sorry
that I wasn't strong enough
to fight the hate
you had for yourself.

Maybe we were just wasting our time.

Or maybe we weren't.

But in the end,
none of it ever really mattered.

Because as it turned out,
we never even had a choice.

If I could. . .

I would trade
a thousand of our yesterdays
for just one more tomorrow.

Because tomorrow might be the day
that you'd decide
you would rather stay and fight for us
instead of walking away.

We were golden,
the color of September.

Wild,
like the wind.

Dancing in circles,
drunk on summer wine.

Believing in forever.

But words can't be unspoken,
and what is gone will never come back.

And we were lost.

Lost in the cold empty days
of that one long winter.

When the world went dark
and we ran out of moments.

When forever ended
and we found our hearts had turned to ice.

When everything got turned upside down
and we couldn't survive the cold.

Right love.
Wrong time.

Never able
to get it together
long enough to do forever.

But never willing
to stop trying.

So reset the clock.

Here we go again.

You were the beginning of my world,
and you were the end of it too.

I seem to have forgotten the rest.

The parts between hello and goodbye,
got lost somewhere in the middle of it all.

But beginnings
and endings
were all that ever really mattered anyway.

Broken but beautiful,
or so they say.

I wander through the wreckage of my life,
searching for peace,
but only seeing madness.

I find myself.
Then I get lost again.

I am a perfect cliché.

Lights.
Camera.
Action.

You play your role.
I'll play mine.

Maybe if we keep pretending,
we will start to actually believe
that we aren't really broken.

So come stand under the lights with me
and we will speak our scripted lies.

The truth never looked good on us anyway.

Life with you
is a maze of complexities.

Hope and truth
are virtual strangers to each other

Wandering aimlessly
through the days
never able to find my way out.

"Who is he?"
(He is my heart.)

"For how long?"
(I've loved him since I was 16 years old.)

"How would you describe your relationship?"
(I've always loved him more than he loved me.)

"How would you describe him?"
(He's broken.)

I guess I'll never know.

Did the cracks in your soul
let the light in,
or the darkness out?

I wish we could find our True North.

So we don't keep getting lost,
while we are learning how to fly.

It's too bad
we don't speak the language of birds.

Take me to the edge of the world.
There is nowhere else for us.

Show me the shadowed places
where sinners and saints come to dance.

We won't tell a soul.

And I promise,
I will gladly pay the price
for our silence.

Those long-ago days
seemed like they would last forever.

We thought we had all the time in the world.

But somehow
when we weren't looking
our time ran out.

Do you ever think of those days?

Do you ever think of me,
in the quiet moments before you fall asleep?

Or did all the memories disappear,
when summer did?

Some old song that I once knew
keeps playing in the back of my mind.

I know the melody.

It's as familiar to me
as the sound of my own breath.

But I seem to have forgotten the words.

They are close though.
So close that I can almost touch them.

But when I reach out
they slip away
and vanish like smoke.

Just like you did,
when you stopped playing that song for me.

I cannot stand the light of day,
where the glare is harsh,
and bright reflections sting my eyes.

I hide from the night's oppressive darkness,
where I can barely breathe
in the heavy desperate air.

I find peace
only in the early gray mornings.

When the fog softens all the sharp corners
and my vision dims, blurring the obvious.

Finally free,
in the fleeting moments
before a broken dawn.

My life in the clouds.

You went away,
forever ago.

But a part of you is still here.
Somewhere.

Words on creased pages.

Out of sight.
Almost out of mind.

Because I closed that book a long time ago.

I put it away on a high shelf,
just out of reach.

But I like to think I can still find you.

Only if I need to though.
And only that one small part of you.

That one small part that you gave to me,
and only me.

The part that you didn't take with you
when you left.

Dried roses.

Pressed between the worn yellowing pages
of my old scrapbook.

Faded photos
in face down frames.

A dusty velvet box
might hold a broken promise ring.

(Or maybe it was just a broken promise?)

This is all I have left
of what never was.

Up and down.
Round and round.

Endless circles.

Bright lights hurt my eyes.
I feel dizzy and weak.

The calliope plays
and painted horses dance.

Stuck on a carousel
that never stops.

When I think of you,
I think of summer.

Shimmering golden days
dipped in strawberry wine.

Driving the backroads with the windows down.

Dashboard drumming.
Singing while the wind stole our voices.

Easy in the world.

Rockstar dreams in the back of your mind.
Forever in the back of mine.

You had to fly.
I gave you a safe place to land.

You wanted me.

I needed you.

And that was never quite enough
for either of us.

When I close my eyes
I can still hear the ocean,
and it reminds me of you.

Back when there were flowers in the sky
and everything that needed to be
was exactly how it was.

I want to go back to that time.

Back to that time when we were magic.

When papers stars rustled in a twilight breeze
and dandelion wishes came true.

Back when life was right
and we were beautiful.

I won't accept
the best of you,
when you can't take
the worst of me.

Please sympathize
with my simple lies.

The truth is found
beyond my eyes.

I apologize.

For chasing invisible monsters
when I should have been chasing you.

The stars hold all my secrets
that I cannot bear to feel.

But can't you see the magic in my madness?

Is it cold where you are now?

Do you miss watching the sun
sink down into the ocean?

Are you wishing for summer?

Do you ever think about where we were then?
Or where I am now?

Do you even know that I'm still here?

Do you ever dream of coming back?

Coming back to me.
To California.

Little moments,
like snowflakes.

Captured and locked away
in the back of my heart.

Sweet mementos,
frozen in time.

Back from when life was easy
and we were all that there ever was.

We were dreamers.

We believed the moon shone brighter
when we stood beneath it,
and we lit up the sky like a meteor shower.

We thought the world knew our names.

But our stars burned too hot,
and everything around us caught fire.

Even after all these years,
I still look for you among the ashes,
and I still wish on the shooting stars.

You came to me that day,
a beautiful but broken boy.

Wearing the scars of your father.
Bearing them as best you could.

(I left my own marks on you, but we laughed
about them later.)

I wish I could have protected you.

Taken away the jagged parts
that cut you so deeply.

Hidden them away inside of me
where they couldn't touch you anymore.

They wouldn't have hurt me very much.

I was always stronger than you.

But I let you keep them.
And I let you go.

Because you asked me to.

I am trying to learn
to find my way
in a life without you.

But I keep getting lost.

Ever since that day
when you let go of my hand,
and walked off in the other direction.

Who I am,
is not who I want to be.

I keep hoping that if I just keep running
I won't ever have to face myself.

And if I ever get to where I'm going,
I might finally forget
where I've been.

Second-hand love stories
written across a galaxy of paper stars.

The words are slowly fading.

Suffocated by silence,
and carried away in a river of silver smoke.

But I will stay here,
in this place,
as long as hope remains.

Even after the stars have gone dark
and blown away.

You can't let loving me
be your reason for staying here.

I know that you love me.

And you need to let that be the reason
you walk away.

Remember me.
If you can.

Remember us.
But only if it doesn't make you feel too sad.

And only if you think
that we were worth remembering.

Even now,
I still find myself
looking back over my shoulder.

Wondering
if you'll still be standing there.
looking back at me.

I am the master of my craft.

Deflecting arrows.
Dodging bullets.

Keeping the hurt quiet.

Because giving pain a voice gives it power.

Silence is my only weapon,
in a war that doesn't belong to me.

The night is crying.

But the stars are still dancing in the sky,
and the world didn't go dark.

So maybe that means
our first good-bye
wasn't meant to be our last.

And maybe giving up
wasn't what was supposed to happen.

What if we really were
meant to do forever?

Maybe the stars really do know best after all.

It's easy to love what's beautiful.

All the bright and shiny things,
perfectly polished,
sitting neatly on a shelf.

So I need you to feel all my sharp edges,
and hold my broken parts in your hands.

Let me take you into the darkness
where the monsters live.

I will show you the dirty, loud, and scary places
where I scream at the night
and the night screams back.

Then we can talk about what love is.

Call it what you will.
Speak of it however you remember it.

Say we were lost.
Say we were magic.
Say we were too young to know any better.

Call us blind.
Call us beautiful.

Say we were reckless and wild,
and that we weren't strong enough
to walk through the fire.

Say that we were the fire.

Say that it never really mattered to you.

Speak of the scars,
but also speak of the stars.

Say it didn't mean anything.

It's all true.
However you choose to remember it.

Call it whatever you want.

I will too.

Because to me,
it was everything.

part two

I lost you to a world
that I could never understand.

And it broke my heart.
But it didn't break me.

I'm not that fragile.

And besides,
I've always preferred chasing madness over fireflies.

Once upon a very long time ago. . .

In a different world
and a different life,
I met a boy who made music.

It was all he knew how to do.

And he played his drums
while my heart kept time.

And that boy gave his songs to me,
because it was all he had to give.

And in return
I gave him my heart.

But he didn't know what to do with it
so he tucked it away in his back pocket.

And when he went away
he took my heart with him.

I never tried to get it back,
because I still had the songs he gave me.

And that's all I ever really needed anyway.

Battles are fought.
Lives are lost.

Life in a war zone.

Step carefully,
for I am surrounded by land mines.

Bullets rain.
You brought the rain.
Your reign will end.

I will throw my white flag into the wind
and I will stand and fight,
and you will remember my name.

Our future
may be written in the stars.

But only the wind
knows the secrets of our past.

My words are my geography.

Finding me.
Defining me.

Mapping the course
of where I came from
and where I am now.

They nourish me.

Soft edges with sharp teeth,
wrapping around me
like a climbing vine seeking the light.

I open my eyes
in the middle of a perfect storm
and speak my truth.

Finally, I'm awake.

You're back.

After all this time,
here you are again.

Our worlds will collide
so brace for impact.

Your heart may be burning now,
but mine has turned to ice.

Fire frees.
But ice will freeze your flames.

And I have become cold
and wickedly harsh.

You can't melt my winter anymore.

I know that loving me
can feel heavy sometimes.

And that the weight of it
might bring you to your knees.

So if the burden ever becomes too much to bear,
please let me go.

So you can stand tall again
and we can both fly free.

I'm not that girl anymore.
The one with darkness inside.

I found comfort
in the blurry brightness of the sun.

It banished the shadows
and melted the ice in my smile.

I have been reborn
into music and light.
and I no longer fear the night.

A heart is heavier when it's broken.
Grief weighs far more than stone.

But I will carry it all proudly,
even though I may stumble sometimes.

Because without that heavy burden,
I would never have learned how to fight.

And if you can't fight,
you can't ever really live.

I see the truth
that lies behind
your cold hard eyes.

You think that you can own the stars.

Pull them from the sky
and lock them away in your glass castle.

Like you thought you could own me.

But I am the stars.

And the stars and I are free.

You can put on your make-believe crown
and hide behind your shiny life.

But you will never know the magic
that comes from dancing with the moon
and loving the wild night.

The game has started.
All my cards are on the table.

You dealt the hand
and I'm calling your bluff.

You are not the king of anything
and my heart is wild.

All in.
I win.

I thought that you had used up
all the good parts of me.

I thought that I was empty.

A hollow seashell
washed up on the sand,
abandoned by the wild tides.

But I find that I don't mind this place.

Because at night the moon comes alive
and it calls the waves to dance.

And everyone knows that shells
hold the echoes of the ocean.

And it turns out
that the very best part of me
is still right here on the shore.

We were a disaster waiting to happen.

Two savage forces, hitting head on
and leaving a trail of wreckage behind us.

But I'm no stranger to the rain,
and I'm not afraid of thunder.

And bullets don't hurt underwater.

So even though you brought your fiercest storms,
I moved on to higher ground.

And when I danced in the dark,
my light shone through clouds
and showed me the way home.

This is for the lost boys,
with their cold eyes and steel hearts.

And for the broken girls,
born in crumbling castles,
dreaming of happily *never* after.

Speak your false prayers
in the darkness if you must,
but don't hide in the shadows,
for the light only speaks with honesty.

Your name may be a lie,
but the truth is rising with the sun.

Let it shine.

My prophecy
is not self-fulfilling.

And even though
my crystal ball is cracked,
I can still see that the path I'm on
will never lead me back
to you.

I heard the truth
in my own silence.

So I took back my voice
the day you walked away.

Sometimes life gets too loud.

And when the weight on my shoulders
seems too heavy to bear,
I find peace underwater.

I float in the quiet darkness.
I don't care that I can't breathe.

Strong currents beckon me out to sea,
but I know that I'm not a mermaid.

So I swim back towards the beach.

Best for me to catch my breath,
and carry my own burden,
and watch the waves from the shore.

"And if I wake before I die . . ."

I promise to remember how I got here,
and that I will keep my eyes wide open this time.

I will understand that sleepwalking
is not the same as living,

And that feeling something,
(anything)
even if it hurts,
is better than feeling nothing at all.

I will lift my eyes
to the midnight skies,
and let you be the moon.

And I will be the wolf,
wild and howling.

And I will wish
on each of the paper stars you hung for me,
even though I know
they might someday blow away.

There I was,
stuck in the middle
of where you left me.

Tangled up in that crazy web you spun.

Trying to make the best
of the very worst of it.

And I learned
that I wasn't as strong
as I wanted to be.

But it turned out
that I wasn't as weak
as you thought I was.

Is this too much?
Or not enough?

Scales tipping back and forth,
something always seems out of balance.

I'm walking on a tightrope
and I'm terrified of falling.

But if I do,
I like to think
you will be there to catch me.

The space between us
gives me comfort.

And I have earned the right to seek it.

Moving through the empty air,
I can dream without sleeping.

Then the quiet brings me back.

And from that dark place,
something beautiful emerges.

Kaleidoscope days.

Dancing inside
brightly colored bits of madness.

Drunk on summer.
Free and wild.

Living in the magic
of our own making.

Whatever makes you feel alive
will take the most ordinary moment
and turn it into something beautiful.

So please don't ever stop believing in magic.

And please don't ever be afraid to live.

Moments are such fragile things.

Delicate.
Like butterfly wings.

Precious yet fleeting,
dancing in the air between us.

But we both know
they can vanish in an instant.

Let's move quietly,
so they don't float away too soon.

I think back to that summer.

That long slow summer,
when we were young
and everything was free and easy.

We would get in my car
and drive to nowhere,
all night long.

And when the sun came up
we'd find ourselves
right back where we started.

And it didn't matter at all.

Because we were seventeen,
and we had all the time in the world to get there.

I know that if I had turned around
and seen you standing there,
my heart would have broken.

So I never once looked back.

I kept moving forward,
even though I was afraid.

Afraid that the very best parts of me
were left behind with you.

It goes like it goes.

The book of us.

Your fiction.
My facts.

So much remained unwritten.

But my pen was mightier than your sword.

I have my own voice
and I told my own story.

And with permanent ink
I wrote my own happy ending.

I knew it was time to walk away,
when I realized that being with you
had become more important
than being myself.

Seventeen.
In between.

Blanket forts
and Saturday morning cartoons.
Giggling like children
years after we weren't.

Loving each other so fiercely,
with everything we had
long before we were ready.

Old enough to know better.
Too young to do any of it right.

But it was perfect.

I admit it.
I may have spun out of control for a while.

But,
I never once crashed.

Please don't apologize
for who you are.

And please don't ever stop
being yourself.

Even if that means,
you will never be the one
for me.

My rear-view mirror has gotten so foggy
that I can't see behind me anymore.

But I know my future lies on the horizon.

So I'll keep looking ahead
and follow the setting sun into tomorrow.

I love myself enough now.

So it's OK
if you don't.

A million memories.

A thousand days
and a thousand miles between us.

You still feel like home to me.

I remember that day.

So long ago,
but it may as well have been yesterday.

The day when you walked away
and everything fell apart.

The day that I broke into a million pieces.

I was so afraid
that I would never be the same again.

And it turns out I was right.
I'm not the same anymore.

But I'm putting myself back together again.
And I think I like what I've become.

Some parts got switched around
and a few edges don't quite line up.

But I can see light
shining through the cracks.

And I know that the bonds
holding it all together
won't break again.

And I am stronger than I was before.
I am better than I was before.

We never really stood a chance.
Because you were never really here.

Your heart was locked away
in the prison of your past.

And it was always too hard for me
to compete with a memory.

So I let you go.
Back to your ghosts.

And I got back to living.

I wish you could have realized
not everything broken
needs to be fixed.

And not everything that's lost
needs saving.

Maybe one day you'll understand
that it was best to let me put myself back together
and to try and find my own way.

And if I do,
maybe I'll find my way
back to you.

I was weak
before I was strong.

A princess without a voice.

Stumbling silently though the gardens
of melancholy would-be kings

Navigating the crumbling architecture
of castles built by sad-eyed boys
with broken souls.

Roses dying on the vine,
before they ever had a chance to bloom.

I was weak
before I was strong.

I was strong
before I was happy.

The cost of growing flowers
for ghosts.

A butterfly with broken wings,
A songbird who's too sad to sing.

But not today.

Today my voice will ring out,
clear and strong.

Then watch me as I fly.

Soaring high
above all the reasons
I shouldn't be able to.

If you are willing to try
just one more time,
I'll show you
that I'm not really made of glass.

And I promise
I won't break this time.

Can you calm the storms
raging inside of me?

Make the thunder whisper,
and convince the crashing waves
to just roll gently to the shore?

Can you quiet the screams inside my head,
and banish the darkness
to keep my nightmares away?

Then please sing me to sleep
and show me what the world looks like
outside of the shadows.

And hold my hand
and let peace bring us home.

Leaving you,
was the hardest thing I've ever done.

But it was the first step
on the journey back to myself.

And losing you,
it broke my heart.

But in the end
I found myself again.

And that's what saved me.

If you choose to love me,
then love me enough to come back,
even if I push you away.

Wrap me tightly in your arms,
and hold on tightly to the fragile thread
that ties me to you.

I promise I won't pull back too hard.

Please walk beside me,
no matter how far I wander,
and understand
that our memories breathe on their own.

A life independent,
separated by the thin veil
of a past we didn't share

Gypsy winds sing of freedom.
But I won't run.

Because it would never be worth the cost
of losing you.

Quiet birds in gilded cages.
Aching wings too weary for flight
(or fight)

Feathers collected
for your many hats.

But some songs can't be silenced.

And feathers can blow away
in a gust of wind.

I am the wind.
I sing.

I see my reflection
in the dirty window.

I must fly.

At long last,
resurrection.

I touch the sky.

I never knew
how strong I was,
until I was able to survive you.

I'm not a little girl anymore,
and I don't believe in fairy tales.

I've never been a princess,
and I've learned how to save myself.

I understand
that armor will tarnish
and lose its shine,
and that even the bravest heroes are flawed.

So please
just hold my hand
as the clock strikes midnight.

Then we can write our own happily ever after.

I want the every day.

Simple and easy.

A gentle touch
to soften the sharp edges of a rough world

Little moments
that pass like whispers,
on lazy Sunday mornings.

A safe place
where I can close my eyes.

A quiet place for my soul to rest.

I was asleep underwater,
for as long as I can remember.

But then you came along,
and you brought the light with you.

It broke through the dark
and called me from my dreams,
when you called out my name.

Now I find myself wide awake,
and I find that I don't mind at all.

The space between
where we once were
and where we are now
is closing.

Time is catching up with itself,
and the past is becoming the future.

Everything is becoming
how it has always been.

And we are exactly where we belong.

Don't ever lose faith in the ordinary,
for it inspires misfits
to become poets.

It all led up to this.

We have lived
a thousand lifetimes.

Everywhere we've been
and everything we've done
has brought us to this place.

And we are finally here,
writing our own love story.

Magic is everywhere.

You just have to believe it
to see it.

All of our monsters were banished
back into the shadows,
when we stopped chasing storms
and stepped out into the light
to find each other.

Life gets so noisy sometimes,
it can drown out our voices.

And sometimes I find myself
running so fast
that I can hardly catch my breath.

But then I see you
out of the corner of my eye.

And I remember
what is worth slowing down for.

And I breathe in the quiet
that is you.

I didn't realize I was lost,
until the day you found me.

It's true,
I was alone.

But solitude has always been easy for me,
and I never minded the quiet.

But then you took my hand
and took me home.

And I knew I had found
where I belonged.

I knew I had found forever
in you.

Even though
I get lost sometimes,
and I don't know which direction I'm going. . .
there is you.

Always,
the weight of you.

Heavy,
yet easy and soft.

An anchor,
but never dragging me down,
only keeping me from drifting away.

And always,
the beacon of light
that guides me home.

We are children of the night,
but not of darkness.

The stars beckon
and we come out to play.

And by the light of the moon
we come alive.

Dancing in the in-between.

The air is alive with magic
that I can feel without seeing.

Little perfect moments.

Wide open spaces
in unfamiliar places.

Tell me where I am?

Frozen in time.
Forever sublime.

That night
when we stood beside the ocean,
the moon was full
and we watched it dance across the water.

And just for a moment
when we closed our eyes,
time stood completely still.

And when we reached up
we found that we could touch the sky.

Sometimes
I catch you looking at me,
like you have never seen me before.

And I wonder
if we have become strangers.

Or maybe we always have been?

But then I see that you know
what you have always known.

And when you smile and take my hand,
I see forever in your eyes.

In the beginning
there was us.

And nothing else mattered.

But life gets messy sometimes
and we are learning
that the world is bigger than we are.

And sometimes we stumble,
and lose our way in the dark.

But in the end
there is light.

And in the end
there is always us.

A life abandoned.

Wearing my history around my neck.
I couldn't breathe.

Never able to see the "bright side"
no matter how hard I tried.

But you stayed with me anyway.

Sitting with me in the dark
so I wouldn't be alone.

Holding my hand
so I wouldn't be afraid.

But nights don't last forever
and morning finally broke through.

And when it did
you walked with me,
out into the light.

And we looked at each other
and smiled up into the sun.

It all comes back
to that single moment.

When we stopped chasing ghosts,
and learned to love each other.

And only then
did we finally start living.

The night we met,
we danced beneath a painted sky
hung with a thousand paper stars.

And for a little while
we made magic in a fairytale world.

But even though
my head may be in the clouds sometimes,
I'm still the girl
with her feet planted firmly on the ground.

And the truth is. . .
even Lost Boys have to grow up sometimes.

And this was never (EVER) Neverland.

So today,
I will touch your hand one last time.

Then I will let you go
and watch you fly away.

Good-bye my sweet Peter Pan.

I hope someday you find yourself.

And if you do,
I hope that you can find your way back to me.

Until then, I will smile
and remember you with love.

And until then,
I'll be sitting right here.

Waiting.

And watching the stars.

Made in the USA
Las Vegas, NV
10 May 2022